INDOORS

ten practical projects

BY ERIKA KNIGHT

credits

Art Direction
Arabella Harris

Photography
Georgina Piper

Styling
Adele & Hélène Adamczewski

Location and Props
Freight HHG

Make Up Artist
Isobel Kennedy

Model
Rosalyn Kennedy

Design Layout
Quail Studio

First published in Great Britain in 2021 by
Quail Publishing Limited
Unit 15, Green Farm, Fritwell, Bicester, Oxfordshire,
OX27 7QU
E-mail: info@quailstudio.co.uk

ISBN: 978-1-8384102-0-9

Printed in the UK

'This isn't about following a lifestyle; this is about living. Observing not only how a home looks but honouring how it makes us feel. Rediscovering our sense of touch. Delighting in the restorative process of creating with our hands. Refined utility pieces, relaxed and unstructured, reflecting the warmth and comfort of our shelter. Simple knits for everyday ease: i n d o o r s'

Ten practical projects to celebrate the warmth and tactility of home.

modern designs *for* slow living.

Projects

stitch throw *pattern page 32*

patchwork blanket *pattern page 34*

sweater *pattern page 36*

cardigan *pattern page 40*

bag *pattern page 44*

lampshade *pattern page 48*

rug *pattern page 50*

pots (plain & bobble)
pattern page 52-55

cushions *pattern page 56-65*

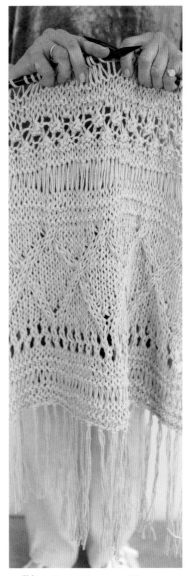

wall hanging *pattern page 66*

A simple shape, like a square throw, is the perfect

place to experiment with texture and colour.

A favourite stitch enlarged and oversized looks new

and different. Throw it over a chair, across

a bed, or around your shoulders.

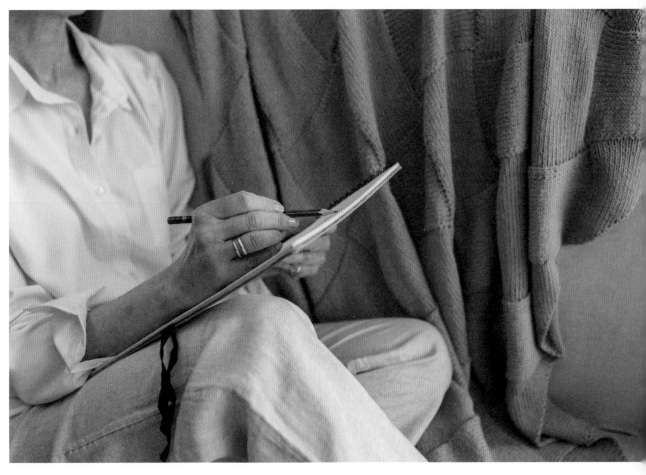

stitch throw

Yarn: Rowan Creative Linen
Colour: Apple 629

A blanket offers more than
an extra layer of warmth.
When we pull it around our
shoulders, or up over our knees,
we feel a sense of protection,
soft armour against the outside
world, security, safety, comfort.

patchwork blanket

Yarn: Rowan Felted Tweed Aran
Colour: Cinnamon 780, Stone 781, Granite 719,
Pine 782, Treacle 783, Carbon 759

Learnt from years of designing, knitting and refining, this is the only sweater you need for everyday ease. External seams for a casual look, made a little oversized for ultimate comfort, and suitable to wear with anything.

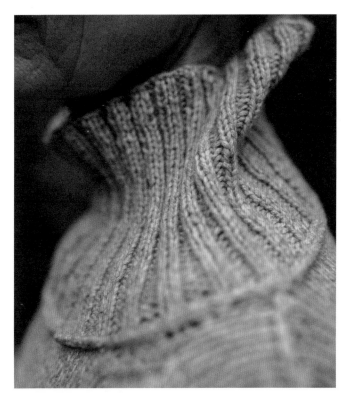

sweater

Yarn: Rowan Softyak DK
Colour: Black 250 / Cream 230

Reliable, lived in, unfussy; the old friend that is there waiting on the back of a chair or on the bedroom floor to transition you from the bustle beyond the front door to the relaxed place, indoors, where you can be yourself and do as you please.

cardigan

Yarn: Rowan Creative Linen
Colour: Natural 621

Storage is a functional necessity, but it needs to work hard in the home. A bag is flexible in its purpose and can be used to transport your day-to-day items with you from room to room as the shape of your day unfolds.

bag

Yarn: Rowan Creative Linen & Felted Tweed Aran
Colour: Straw 622, True Black 653 & Cinnamon 780

lampshade

Yarn: Rowan Kidsilk Haze
Colour: Jelly 597

Levels and layers are important in creating a cocooning home. When you sit down in your favourite armchair or take a seat at the table, your eye is drawn upwards. Fill spaces with objects that are beautiful to you.

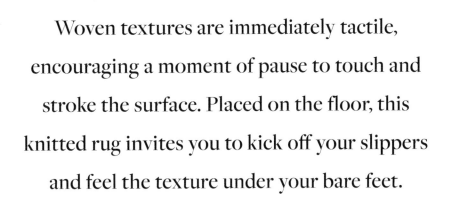

Woven textures are immediately tactile, encouraging a moment of pause to touch and stroke the surface. Placed on the floor, this knitted rug invites you to kick off your slippers and feel the texture under your bare feet.

rug

Yarn: Rowan Creative Linen
Colour: Natural 621

No matter the size of the space you call home, bringing the outside indoors in the form of a plant has many beneficial effects on your mood. Made in natural fibres, this pot complements the botanical and is biodegradable, too.

pots

Yarn: Rowan Creative Linen
Colour: Natural 621

Ubiquitous in adding layers of new texture, colour and interest to a tired chair or forgotten corner, you can never have too many cushions. Play with stripes and scale to use up yarn scraps, and finish with a fabric back.

cushions

Yarn: Rowan Creative Linen, Felted Tweed Aran & Big Wool
Colour: Natural 621, Straw 622, True Black 653 &
Cinnamon 780, Treacle 783 & Cactus 083

A sampler for stitch texture, experiment with scale and tension. Make a feature of your handcrafts and add surface texture to your home.

wall hanging

Yarn: Rowan Creative Linen
Colour: Natural 621

patterns

stitch throw

A square throw knitted in an exaggerated trellis stitch with raw edges.

Measurements
One size
Approx. 120cm x 120cm

Materials
Rowan Creative Linen
50% Cotton, 50% Linen
Approx. 200m per 100g hank
Quantity: 8 hanks (photographed in Apple 629)
4mm circular needles with 100cm length wire
Stitch markers
Large-eyed, blunt-tipped sewing needle
Note: Yarn amounts given are based on average requirements and are approximate.

Tension
19 sts and 26 rows to 10cm, meas over pattern using 4mm needles. Change needle size as necessary to ensure the correct tension.

Notes
This pattern uses circular needles to work in rows. (See p.70)

Inc in first st – knit into front and back of first st.
Picking up stitches with WS facing – with the WS of work facing, insert the RH needle through the edge of the fabric from **back to front,** wind yarn around the needle and draw the loop through, forming a stitch on the RH needle.
Cont in this way until the required number of stitches is on the RH needle.

Abbreviations
See p.70.

Make

Large trellis pattern multiple of 24 sts for this throw.

Using 4mm needles, cast on 144 sts loosely and place markers after every 24 sts. These mark the base triangles and can be removed when the base triangles are completed.

Base triangles

*P2 (WS), turn and K2, turn and P3, turn and K3, turn and P4, turn and K4, cont in this way working 1 more st on every WS row until the row 'turn and P24' has been worked. (This completes the first triangle over 24 sts.) Rep from * to end.

First row of rectangles (with edge triangles)

K2, turn and P2, turn, inc in first st, K2tog tbl, turn and P3, turn, inc in first st, K1, K2tog tbl, turn and P4, turn, inc in first st, K2, K2tog tbl, turn and P5, turn, inc in first st, K3, K2tog tbl, turn and P6, cont in this way working one more st on every RS row until the row 'inc in first st, K21, K2tog tbl' has been worked. (1 edge triangle complete) Then cont as foll:
*With the RS facing, pick up and K24 sts evenly along edge of next base triangle [turn and P24, turn and K23, K2tog tbl] 24 times (1 rectangle complete). Rep from * to edge of last triangle.
With the RS facing, pick up and K24 sts along edge of last triangle, turn and P2tog, P22 turn and K23, turn and P2tog, P21, turn. Cont in this way until 'turn and K2' has been worked, turn and P2tog (1 st remains on RH needle and edge triangle is complete).

Second row of rectangles

Continuing from the st on RH needle, with the WS facing, pick up and P23 sts evenly along edge of triangle just worked, (24 sts on RH needle), [turn and K24, turn and P23, P2tog] 24 times, then cont as foll:
*With the WS facing, pick up and P24 sts evenly along side edge of next rectangle, [turn and K24, turn and P23, P2tog] 24 times; rep from * to end.

Third row of rectangles

As first row but picking up sts along side edge of rectangles instead of triangles.
Rep second and third rows of rectangle until work meas approx. 120cm from the cast-on ending after completing a third row.

Final row of triangles

*Cont on from st on RH needle, with the WS facing, pick up and P23 sts evenly along edge of triangle just worked, turn and K24, turn and P2tog, P21, P2tog, turn and K23, turn and P2tog, P20, P2tog, turn and K22, turn.
Cont in this way, working one st less on every WS row until the row 'turn and K3' has been worked, turn and [P2tog] twice, turn and K2, turn and P1, P2tog, P1, turn and K3, turn and P3tog; rep from * but pick up sts along side edge of rectangle instead of triangle. Fasten off rem st.

Finish

Weave in any ends in and out of the sts on the WS of the work. Choose a flat padded surface or blocking board, pin work out to measurements. Cover with a damp cloth and gently steam. Leave to dry flat.

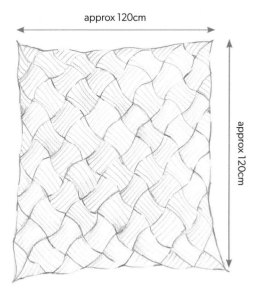

approx 120cm

approx 120cm

patchwork blanket

A refined version of the traditional patchwork blanket worked using the intarsia technique rather than individual squares sewn together. Knitted in stocking stitch and reverse stocking stitch to make the blanket reversible, with added interest in the colour change rows.

Measurements
One size
Approx. 120cm x 120cm

Materials
Rowan Felted Tweed Aran
50% Wool, 25% Viscose, 25% Alpaca
Approx. 87m per 50g ball
Quantity:
A 3 balls (photographed in Cinnamon 780)
B 3 balls (photographed in Carbon 759)
C 3 balls (photographed in Treacle 783)
D 3 balls (photographed in Pine 782)
E 3 balls (photographed in Granite 719)
F 3 balls (photographed in Stone 781)
5mm circular needles with 100cm length wire
Large-eyed, blunt-tipped sewing needle
Note: Yarn amounts given are based on average requirements and are approximate.

Tension
16 sts and 23 rows to 10cm, meas over St st using 5mm needles. Change needle size as necessary to ensure the correct tension.

Notes
This pattern uses circular needles to work in rows. (See p.70)

This blanket is worked in squares of St st and Rev St st, using the intarsia method, following the diagram and changing stitch and colour as indicated. Use a separate ball for each square and twist the yarns on the WS of the work when changing colour to avoid a hole.

All squares using colour **F** are Rev St st.
Working with colour F
On first row of squares:
Row 1 (RS): Lay tail end (approx. 15cm) of **F** at the back of the work and P32**F**.
(RS): K32 **F**, bring yarn forward and twist with **E** to avoid holes.
Next row and cont as above: Twist col **F** with adjoining col on the back of work, then bring col **F** to the front to work the Rev St st.

Working col **F** (Rev St st square) in between St st squares.
RS: Twist col **F** and adjoining col on the back of work, bring col **F** forward, P32**F**, bring yarn back to twist with next colour.
WS: Twist the yarns together on the WS of work and bring col **F** to the front, K32**F**, bring yarn **F** back to twist with next colour.

Abbreviations
See p.70.

Make
Using 5mm needles and yarn **F**, cast on 192 sts and work as foll:

First section of squares
Row 1 (RS): K32**A**, K32**B**, K32**C**, K32**D**, K32**E**, P32**F** (see above note about working with col **F**).
Row 2: K32**F**, P32**E**, P32**D**, P32**C**, P32**B**, P32**A**.
These 2 rows set the squares for the first section. Rep last 2 rows 22 times more. 46 rows in total. The squares should meas 20cm from the cast-on edge.
Cont working from the diagram until all sections are completed, ending with RS facing for next row.
Change to **B** and K across all sts.
Cast off in purl using **B**.
Fasten off.

Finish
Weave any ends in and out of the sts on the WS of the work, leaving some ends loose as an optional design feature.
Choose a flat padded surface or blocking board and pin work out to measurements. Cover with a damp cloth and gently steam. Leave to dry flat.

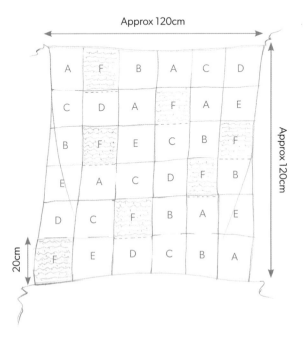

Approx 120cm

Approx 120cm

A	F	B	A	C	D
C	D	A	F	A	E
B	F	E	C	B	F
E	A	C	D	F	B
D	C	F	B	A	E
F	E	D	C	B	A

20cm

sweater

A long-sleeve drop-shoulder sweater, knitted in stocking stitch with 2 x 2 rib welts, cuffs and collar. The stitches are picked up on the right side of the garment at the welts, armhole and neck to create an external seam detail. The back shoulder is shaped with a fully fashioned technique and shoulders are finished with a three-needle cast-off on the outside. The sleeves are picked up at the armhole and worked down to the cuffs. Finished with a patch pocket hand stitched into position to detail.

Measurements

	1	2	3	4	5	6	7	8	9	
Finished chest:										
	104	115	125	136	144	155	165	176	184	cm
Length:										
	61	63	65	67	69	71	73	75	77	cm
Sleeve underarm:										
	44	44	44	44	42	42	42	40	40	cm

Note: Design shown in photos is a size 2. Model is UK size 8, height 5'3".

Materials

Rowan Softyak DK
76% Cotton, 15% Yak, 9% Nylon
Approx. 135m per 50g ball
Quantity: 11(12:13:14:15:17:18:19:21) balls
(photographed in Cream 230 and Black 250)
4mm needles
3.75mm circular needle with 60cm length wire
Stitch markers
Stitch holders
Large-eyed, blunt-tipped sewing needle
Note: Yarn amounts given are based on average requirements and are approximate.

Tension

22 sts and 30 rows to 10cm, meas over St st using 4mm needles. Change needle size as necessary to ensure the correct tension.

Abbreviations

See p.70.

Special abbreviations

Skpo slip 1 st knitwise, K1, pass slipped stitch over.

Make

Back

Using 4mm needles, cast on 114(126:138:150:158:170:182: 194:202) sts and work in rib as foll:

Row 1 (RS): [K2, P2] to last 2 sts, K2.

Row 2: [P2, K2] to last 2 sts, P2.

Rep last 2 rows until work meas 7.5(7.5:7.5:7.5:8:8:8:8.5:8.5)cm from the cast-on ending with RS facing for next row.

Cast off in rib.

Create an outside seam as foll:

With **WS** facing, working 2 rows below the cast-off edge of rib, pick up and K 114(126:138:150:158:170:182:194:202) sts. Beg with a K row, cont in St st until work meas 53(55:57:59:61:63:65:67:69)cm from the cast-on, ending with RS facing for next row, placing markers at 35(36:37:38:39:40:41:42:43)cm to mark start of armholes.

Shape shoulders

Next row: K to last 3(3:4:4:5:5:6:6:7) sts, wrap next st and turn.

Next row: P to last 3(3:4:4:5:5:6:6:7) sts, wrap next st and turn.

Next row: K to last 6(6:8:8:10:10:12:12:13) sts, wrap next st and turn.

Next row: P to last 6(6:8:8:10:10:12:12:13) sts, wrap next st and turn.

Next row: K to last 9(9:12:12:15:15:18:18:19) sts, wrap next st and turn.

Next row: P to last 9(9:12:12:15:15:18:18:19) sts, wrap next st and turn.

Next row: K to last 12(12:16:16:20:20:23:24:25) sts, wrap next st and turn.

Next row: P to last 12(12:16:16:20:20:23:24:25) sts, wrap next st and turn.

Next row: K to last 15(15:20:20:24:25:28:30:31) sts, wrap next st and turn.

Next row: P to last 15(15:20:20:24:25:28:30:31) sts, wrap next st and turn.

Next row: K to last 18(18:24:24:28:30:33:36:37) sts, wrap next st and turn.

Next row: P to last 18(18:24:24:28:30:33:36:37) sts, wrap next st and turn.

Next row: K to last 21(21:27:28:32:35:38:42:43) sts, wrap next st and turn.

Next row: P to last 21(21:27:28:32:35:38:42:43) sts, wrap next st and turn.

Next row: K to last 23(24:30:32:36:40:43:48:49) sts, wrap next st and turn.

Next row: P to last 23(24:30:32:36:40:43:48:49) sts, wrap next st and turn.

Next row: K to last 25(27:33:36:40:45:48:54:55) sts, wrap next st and turn.

Next row: P to last 25(27:33:36:40:45:48:54:55) sts, wrap next st and turn.

Next row: K to last 27(30:36:40:44:49:53:59:61) sts, wrap next st and turn.

Next row: P to last 27(30:36:40:44:49:53:59:61) sts, wrap next st and turn.

Next row: K to last 29(33:39:44:48:53:58:64:67) sts, wrap next st and turn.

Next row: P to last 29(33:39:44:48:53:58:64:67) sts, wrap next st and turn.

Next row: K2(3:3:3:4:4:4:5:5:6), turn.

Next row: P to end of row, picking up the wraps as you work. Cut yarn leaving a long end.

Slip these 31(36:42:48:52:57:63:69:73) sts onto a holder for the shoulder.

With RS of work facing, rejoin yarn to rem sts, cast off centre 52(54:54:54:54:56:56:56:56) sts and K to end of row, picking up the wraps as you work.

Cut yarn leaving a long end.

Slip these 31(36:42:48:52:57:63:69:73) sts onto a holder for the shoulder.

Front

Work as back until work meas 55(56:58:60:61:63:65:66:68)cm from the cast-on, ending with RS facing for next row, placing markers at 35(36:37:38:39:40:41:42:43)cm to show start of armholes.

Shape neck

Next row: K50(55:61:67:71:76:82:88:92), turn and leave rem sts on a holder.

Cast off 4 sts at beg of next and foll 2 alt rows. 38(43:49:55:59:64:70:76:80) sts.

Next row (dec): K to last 5 sts, skpo, K3. 37(42:48:54:58:63:69:75:79) sts.

Next row (dec): P3, P2tog tbl, P to end of row. 36(41:47:53:57:62:68:74:78) sts.

Dec 1 st at neck edge as above on next 5(5:5:5:5:3:3:3:3) rows, then on foll 0(0:0:0:0:2:2:2:2) alt rows. 31(36:42:48:52:57:63:69:73) sts.

Cont straight until work meas 61(63:65:67:69:71:73:75:77)cm from the cast-on, ending with RS facing for next row.
Cut yarn leaving a long end.
Slip these 31(36:42:48:52:57:63:69:73) sts onto a holder for the shoulder.
With RS of work facing, rejoin yarn to rem sts, cast off centre 14(16:16:16:16:18:18:18:18) sts and K to end of row. 50(55:61:67:71:76:82:88:92) sts.
Next row: P.
Cast off 4 sts at beg of next and 2 foll alt rows. 38(43:49:55:59:64:70:76:80) sts.
Next row: P.
Next row (dec): K3, K2tog, K to end of row. 37(42:48:54:58:63:69:75:79) sts.
Next row (dec): P to last 5 sts, P2tog, P3. 36(41:47:53:57:62:68:74:78) sts.
Dec 1 st at neck edge, as above, on next 5(5:5:5:5:3:3:3:3) rows, then on foll 0(0:0:0:0:2:2:2:2) alt rows. 31(36:42:48:52:57:63:69:73) sts.
Cont straight until work meas 61(63:65:67:69:71:73:75:77)cm from the cast-on, ending with WS facing for next row.
Cut yarn leaving a long end.
Slip these 31(36:42:48:52:57:63:69:73) sts onto a holder for the shoulder.
Join both shoulders using the three-needle cast-off method with WS of work facing so that the seam is on the outside of your work.

Sleeves knitted from the top down with an outside seam along the armhole and the dec are worked as foll:
RS (dec): K3, K2tog, K to last 5 sts, K2tog tbl, K3.
WS (dec): P3, P2tog tbl, P to last 5 sts, P2tog, P3.
With **WS** of work facing, pick up and K100(104:108:112:116: 122:126:130:134) sts evenly between armhole stitch markers.
Beg with a K row, work 4 rows St st.
Dec as above on every foll 7th(6th:6th:5th:5th:5th:4th:4th:4th) row until 70(80:84:98:90:82:108:82:86) sts, then on every foll 0(7th:7th:6th:6th:0:5th:0:0) row until 0(70:74:74:78:0:82:0:0) sts. 70(70:74:74:78:82:82:82:86) sts.
Cont straight until sleeve meas 37(37:37:37:35:35:35:33:33)cm from the pick-up.
Cast off.

Create an outside seam as foll:
With **WS** of work facing, pick up and K 70(70:74:74:78:82:82:82:86) sts along the cast-off edge of the sleeve, working 2 rows below the cast-off.
Cont in rib as foll:
Next row (RS): [K2, P2] to last 2 sts, K2.
Next row: [P2, K2] to last 2 sts, P2.
Rep last 2 rows until rib meas 9cm for all sizes.
Cast off in rib.

Collar
Using 3.75mm circular needle and **WS** of work facing, pick up and K 52(54:54:54:54:56:56:56:56) sts along back neck, 23(25:25:25:25:27:27:27:27) sts down side neck, 14(16:16:16:16:18:18:18:18) sts across centre front and 23(25:25:25:25:27:27:27:27) sts up side neck, placing a marker to show start of round. 112(120:120:120:120:128:128: 128:128) sts. Work in rounds as foll:
Next round: [K2, P2] to end of round.
Rep this round until rib meas 13cm from pick up, ending at marker.
Cast off in rib.

Pocket - slip first st of every row.
Using 4mm needles, cast on 33(35:35:35:37:37:37:39:39) sts and beg with a K row cont in St st until pocket meas 16(17:17:17:18:18:18:19:19)cm from the cast-on, ending with RS facing for next row.
Cast off.

Finish
Weave any ends in and out of the sts on the WS of the work.
Choose a flat padded surface or blocking board and pin work out to measurements. Cover with a damp cloth and gently steam on reverse, avoiding ribbing. Leave to dry flat.
Join side and sleeve seams, leaving the rib hem on both sides open to give a little vent detail.
Place cast-on edge of pocket approx. 15(16:17:18:18:19:20:20:21)cm from the cast-on edge of the hem and 6(7.5:10:13:13:16:18:19:21)cm in from the righthand side edge of the sweater. Pin into position and sew on securely using back stitch.

52 (57.5: 62.5: 68: 72: 77.5: 82.5: 88: 92)cm

44 (44: 44: 44: 42: 42: 42: 40: 40)cm

61 (63: 65: 67: 69: 71: 73: 75: 77)cm

cardigan

A relaxed-fit, drop-shoulder cardigan knitted in stocking stitch with outside seams at rib edges and armholes and two patch pockets to detail. The back shoulder is shaped with a fully fashioned technique and shoulders are finished with a three-needle cast-off on the outside. The button bands are worked integrally in with the front pieces and the sleeves are picked up at the armhole and worked down to the cuffs to give a neat finish.

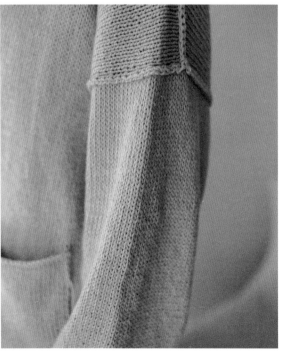

Measurements

1	2	3	4	5	6	7	8	9	
Finished chest:									
106	116	126	136	146	156	166	176	186	cm
Length:									
61	63	65	67	69	71	73	75	77	cm
Sleeve underarm:									
44	44	44	44	42	42	42	40	40	cm

Note: Design shown in photos is a size 2. Model is UK size 8, height 5'3".

Materials

Rowan Creative Linen
50% Cotton, 50% Linen
Approx. 200m per 100g hank
Quantity: 7(7:8:9:9:10:11:11:12) hanks
(photographed in Natural 621)
4mm and 4.5mm needles
Stitch markers
Stitch holders
5 buttons with 2cm diameter
Large-eyed, blunt-tipped sewing needle
Note: Yarn amounts given are based on average requirements and are approximate.

Tension

21 sts and 28 rows to 10cm, meas over St st using 4.5mm needles. Change needle size as necessary to ensure the correct tension.

Abbreviations

See p.70.

Make

Back
Using 4.5mm needles, cast on 111(121:133:143:153:163:175: 185:195) sts and work in rib as foll:
Row 1 (RS): [K1, P1] to last st, K1.
Row 2: [P1, K1] to last st, P1.
Rep last 2 rows until rib meas 7(7:7:7:8:8:8:9:9)cm from the cast-on, ending with RS facing for next row.
Cast off in rib.
Create outside seam as foll:
With **WS** of work facing, pick up and 111(121:133:143: 153:163:175:185:195) sts working through 2 rows below the cast-off. Beg with a K row, cont in St st until work meas 53(55:57:59:61:63:65:67:69)cm from the cast-on, ending with RS facing for next row, placing markers at 35(36:37:38:39:40:41:42:43)cm to mark start of armholes.
Shoulder shaping
Next row: K to last 4(4:4:5:5:6:6:6:7) sts, wrap next st and turn.
Next row: P to last 4(4:4:5:5:6:6:6:7) sts, wrap next st and turn.
Next row: K to last 8(8:8:10:10:12:12:12:14) sts, wrap next st and turn.
Next row: P to last 8(8:8:10:10:12:12:12:14) sts, wrap next st and turn.
Next row: K to last 11(12:12:15:15:17:18:18:21) sts, wrap next st and turn.
Next row: P to last 11(12:12:15:15:17:18:18:21) sts, wrap next st and turn.
Next row: K to last 14(16:16:20:20:22:24:24:28) sts, wrap next st and turn.
Next row: P to last 14(16:16:20:20:22:24:24:28) sts, wrap next st and turn.
Next row: K to last 17(20:20:25:25:27:30:30:35) sts, wrap next st and turn.
Next row: P to last 17(20:20:25:25:27:30:30:35) sts, wrap next st and turn.
Next row: K to last 20(24:24:29:30:32:36:36:41) sts, wrap next st and turn.
Next row: P to last 20(24:24:29:30:32:36:36:41) sts, wrap next st and turn.
Next row: K to last 23(28:28:33:35:37:42:42:47) sts, wrap next st and turn.
Next row: P to last 23(28:28:33:35:37:42:42:47) sts, wrap next st and turn.
Next row: K to last 26(31:32:37:40:42:48:48:53) sts, wrap next st and turn.

Next row: P to last 26(31:32:37:40:42:48:48:53) sts, wrap next st and turn.
Next row: K to last 29(34:36:41:45:47:53:54:59) sts, wrap next st and turn.
Next row: P to last 29(34:36:41:45:47:53:54:59) sts, wrap next st and turn.
Next row: K to last 32(37:40:45:49:52:58:60:65) sts, wrap next st and turn.
Next row: P to last 32(37:40:45:49:52:58:60:65) sts, wrap next st and turn.
Next row: K to last 35(40:44:49:53:57:63:66:71) sts, wrap next st and turn.
Next row: P to last 35(40:44:49:53:57:63:66:71) sts, wrap next st and turn.
Next row: K3(3:4:4:4:5:5:6:6), turn.
Next row: P to end of row, picking up the wraps as you work.
Cut yarn leaving a long end.
Slip these 38(43:48:53:57:62:68:72:77) sts onto a holder for the shoulder.
With RS of work facing, slip centre 35(35:37:37:39:39:39:41:41) sts onto a holder.
Rejoin yarn to rem sts and K to end of row, picking up the wraps as you work.
Cut yarn leaving a long end.
Slip these 38(43:48:53:57:62:68:72:77) sts onto a holder for the shoulder.
Right front
Using 4.5mm needles, cast on 61(67:73:77:83:87:93:99:103) sts and work in rib as foll:
Row 1 (RS): [P1, K1] to last st, P1.
Row 2: [K1, P1] to last st, K1.
Rep last 2 rows until rib meas 7(7:7:7:8:8:8:9:9)cm from the cast-on, ending with RS facing for next row.
Cast off in rib.
Create outside seam as foll:
With **WS** of work facing, pick up and K 61(67:73:77:83:87:93:99:103) sts, working through 2 rows below the cast-off and work as foll:
Next row (RS): [P1, K1] four times, P1, K to end of row.
Next row: P to last 9 sts, rib as set.
Rep last 2 rows until work meas 33(35:37:38:40:42:44:45:47)cm from cast-on, ending with RS facing for next row.
Shape front neck – the decreases are worked as foll:
RS row dec – Rib 9 sts as set, K3, K2tog, K to end of row.
WS row dec – P to last 14 sts, P2tog, P3, rib as set to end of row.

Dec as above on next and every foll 6th(5th:5th:6th:5th:5th:5th:5th:5th) row until 53(52:59:69:70:71:77:86:86) sts, then on every foll 5th(0:4th:5th:4th 0: 0: 4th: 0) row until 47(0:57:62:66:0:0:81:-) sts.
47(52:57:62:66:71:77:81:86) sts.
Cont straight with rib edge until front meas 61(63:65:67:69:71:73:75:77)cm from the cast-on edge, ending with RS facing for next row, placing marker at side edge when work meas 35(36:37:38:39:40:41:42:43)cm from cast-on to mark armhole.
Next row: Cast off 9 sts in rib, K to end of row.
Cut yarn leaving a long end.
Slip these 38(43:48:53:57:62:68:72:77) sts onto a holder for the shoulder.
Mark 5 buttonholes on right front as foll:
First buttonhole 3.25cm from cast-on.
Fifth buttonhole 1cm before start of neck shaping.
Three buttonholes evenly spaced between.

Left front
Using 4.5mm needles, cast on 61(67:73:77:83:87:93:99:103) sts and work in rib as foll:
Row 1 (RS): [P1, K1] to last st, P1.
Row 2: [K1, P1] to last st, K1.
Rep last 2 rows 3 times more.
Next row (buttonhole): Patt as set to last 9 sts, P1, K1, K2tog, yo twice, K2tog, rib to end.
Next row: Rib 4 sts as set, P into first yo, P into back of second yo, rib to end.
Rep last 2 rows until rib meas 7(7:7:7:8:8:8:9:9)cm from the cast-on, ending with RS facing for next row. Don't forget to work buttonholes where marked.
Cast off in rib.
Create outside seam as foll:
With **WS** of work facing, pick up and K 61(67:73:77:83:87:93:99:103) sts, working through 2 rows below the cast-off and work as foll:
Next row: K to last 9 sts, rib as set.
Next row: Rib 9 sts as set, P to end of row.
Rep last 2 rows until work meas 33(35:37:38:40:42:44:45:47)cm from cast-on, ending with RS facing for next row. DON'T FORGET TO WORK THE BUTTONHOLES WHERE MARKED.
Shape front neck - the neck decreases are worked as foll:
RS row dec - K to last 14 sts, K2tog tbl, K3, rib to end.

WS row dec - Rib 9 sts as set, P3, P2tog tbl, P to end of row.
Dec as above on next and every foll 6th(5th:5th:6th:5th:5th:5th:5th:5th) row until 53(52:59:69:70:71:77:86:86) sts, then on every foll 5th(0:4th:5th:4th 0: 0: 4th: 0) row until 47(0:57:62:66:0:0:81:0) sts. 47(52:57:62:66:71:77:81:86) sts.
Cont straight with rib edge until front meas 61(63:65:67:69:71:73:75:77)cm from the cast-on edge, ending with WS facing for next row, placing marker at side edge when work meas 35(36:37:38:39:40:41:42:43)cm from cast-on to mark armhole.
Next row: Cast off 9 sts in rib, P to end of row.
Cut yarn leaving a long end.
Slip these 38(43:48:53:57:62:68:72:77) sts onto a holder for the shoulder.
Join both shoulders using the three-needle cast-off method, with WS of work tog so that the seam is on the outside of your work.

Sleeves knitted from the top down with an outside seam along the armhole and the dec are worked as foll:
RS dec: K3, K2tog, K to last 5 sts, K2tog tbl, K3.
WS dec: P3, P2tog tbl, P to last 5 sts P2tog, P3.
Using 4.5mm needles and with **WS** of work facing, pick up and K 95(99:103:107:111:115:119:123:129) sts evenly between armhole markers and beg with a K row, work 4 rows St st.

Dec as above at both ends of next and every foll 6th(6th:5th:4th:4th:4th:3rd:3rd:3rd) row until 89(67:77:101:95:75:109:113:75) sts, then on every foll 7th(0:6th:5th:5th:5th:4th:4th:0) row until 67(0:67:67:71:71:71:75:0) sts.
67(67:67:67:71:71:71:75:75) sts.
Cont straight until sleeve meas 35(35:35:35:33:33:33:31:31)cm from pick up, ending with RS facing for next row.
Cast off.
Create outside seam as foll:
With WS of work facing, pick up and K 67(67:67:67:71:71:71:75:75) sts, working through 2 rows below the cast-off, and work in rib as foll:
Row 1 (RS): [K1, P1] to last st, K1.
Row 2: [P1, K1] to last st, P1.
Rep last 2 rows until rib meas 9cm, ending with RS facing for next row.
Cast off in rib.

Back neckband

Using 4mm needles and RS of work facing, pick up and K4 sts down right back neck, K 35(35:37:37:39:39:39:41:41) sts from centre back st holder and pick up and K4 sts up left back neck. 43(43:45:45:47:47:47:49:49) sts.
Work in rib as foll:
Row 1: [K1, P1] to last st, K1.
Row 2: [P1, K1] to last st, P1.
Rep last 2 rows 4 times more.
Cast off in rib.

Pockets make 2. Slip the first st of every row.
Using 4.5mm needles, cast on 32(32:32:32:34:34:34:36:36) sts and beg with a K row, work in St st until pocket meas 16(16:16:16:17:17:17:18:18)cm from the cast-on, ending with RS facing for next row. Cast off.

Finish

Weave any ends in and out of the sts on the WS of the work. Choose a flat padded surface or blocking board and pin work out to measurements. Cover with a damp cloth and gently steam on reverse, avoiding ribbing. Leave to dry flat.
Join side and sleeve seams.
Place cast-on edge of pockets approx. 10(10:11:11:12:13:13:14:15)cm from the cast-on edge of the hem and approx. 7(8:9:10:11:14:15:17:19)cm in from the side edges of the cardigan, or as desired. Pin into position and sew on securely using back stitch, leaving optional loose ends to detail.
Sew on buttons to match buttonholes.
Join neckband to front bands.

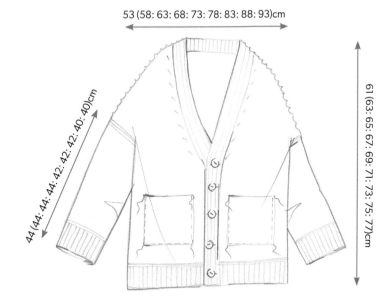

53 (58: 63: 68: 73: 78: 83: 88: 93)cm

44 (44: 44: 44: 42: 42: 42: 40: 40)cm

61 (63: 65: 67: 69: 71: 73: 75: 77)cm

bag

A bag knitted in the round with a circular base, then worked in rows to create long handles to easily go over the shoulder. Knitted in bands of stitch and yarn textures.

Measurements
One size
Approx. 34cm in diameter x 35cm tall

Materials
Rowan Creative Linen
50% Cotton, 50% Linen
Approx. 200m per 100g hank
Quantity:
A 3 hanks (photographed in Straw 622)
B 1 hank (photographed in True Black 653)
Rowan Felted Tweed Aran
50% Wool, 25% Viscose, 25% Alpaca
Approx. 87m per 50g ball
C 1 ball (photographed in Cinnamon 780)
4.5mm and 5mm circular needles with 60cm length wire
Stitch marker
Stitch holder
Approx. 75cm x 120cm linen fabric for lining
Large-eyed, blunt-tipped sewing needle
Note: Yarn amounts given are based on average requirements and are approximate.

Tension
21 sts and 28 rows to 10cm, meas over St st using 4.5mm needles. Change needle size as necessary to ensure the correct tension.

Note
This pattern uses circular needles to work in rows. (See p.70) The magic loop technique is used for the base. (See p.70)

Abbreviations
See p.70.

Special abbreviations
kfb knit into front and back of next st.

Make

Using 4.5mm circular needles and **A**, cast on 8 sts, place a marker to show start of round and, making sure that the cast-on row is not twisted, work in rounds as foll:

Round 1: K.
Round 2: kfb into each st. 16 sts.
Round 3: K.
Round 4: [K1, kfb] to end of round. 24 sts.
Round 5: K.
Round 6: [K2, kfb] to end of round. 32 sts.
Round 7: K.
Round 8: [K3, kfb] to end of round. 40 sts.
Round 9: K.
Round 10: [K4, kfb] to end of round. 48 sts.
Round 11: K.
Round 12: [K5, kfb] to end of round. 56 sts.
Round 13: K.
Round 14: [K6, kfb] to end of round. 64 sts.
Round 15: K.
Round 16: [K7, kfb] to end of round. 72 sts.
Round 17: K.
Round 18: [K8, kfb] to end of round. 80 sts.
Round 19: K.
Round 20: [K9, kfb] to end of round. 88 sts.
Round 21: K.
Round 22: [K10, kfb] to end of round. 96 sts.
Round 23: K.
Round 24: [K11, kfb] to end of round. 104 sts.
Round 25: K.
Round 26: [K12, kfb] to end of round. 112 sts.
Round 27: K.
Round 28: [K13, kfb] to end of round. 120 sts.
Round 29: K.
Round 30: [K14, kfb] to end of round. 128 sts.
Round 31: K.
Round 32: [K15, kfb] to end of round. 136 sts.
Round 33: K.
Round 35: [K16, kfb] to end of round. 144 sts.
Round 36: K.
Round 37: [K17, kfb] to end of round. 152 sts.
Round 38: K.
Round 39: [K18, kfb] to end of round. 160 sts.
Round 40: K.
Round 41: [K19, kfb] to end of round. 168 sts.
Round 42: K.
Round 43: [K20, kfb] to end of round. 176 sts.
Round 44: K.

Round 45: [K21, kfb] to end of round. 184 sts.
Round 46: K.
Round 47: [K22, kfb] to end of round. 192 sts.
Round 48: K.

Cont in broken rib patt as foll:
Round 1: [K1, P1] to end of round.
Round 2: K.
Rep last 2 rounds 10 times more.
Work 3 rounds K.
Change to 5mm needles and work zig zag patt using **A** and **B** as indicated. All sts are K.
Round 1: [2**A**, 1**B**] to end of round.
Round 2: [1**B**, 3**A**, 1**B**, 1**A**] to end of round.
Round 3: [1**A**, 1**B**, 1**A**, 1**B**, 2**A**] to end of round.
Rep last 3 rounds five times more.
Change to 4.5mm needles and **A** work as foll:
3 rounds K.
1 round P.
3 rounds K.
Change to **C** and work 7 rounds P.
Change to **A** and work 3 rounds K.
Change to **B** and work 1 round P.
Change to **A** and work 3 rounds K, inc 4 sts evenly on last round. 196 sts.
*Cont in rows on the first 98 sts in herringbone patt in A as foll:

Special abbreviations

Sl slip stitch purlwise.
Wyif with yarn in front.
Wyib with yarn in back.

Row 1 (RS): K2, [sl2 wyif, K2] to end of row.
Row 2: P1, [sl2 wyib, P2] rep to last st, P1.
Row 3: Sl2 wyif, [K2, sl2 wyif] to end of row.
Row 4: P3, [sl2 wyib, P2] to last 3 sts, sl2 wyib, P1.
Row 5: K2, [sl2 wyif, K2] to end of row.
Row 6: P1, [sl2 wyib, P2] rep to last st, P1.
Row 7: Sl2 wyif, [K2, sl2 wyif] to end of row.
Row 8: P3, [sl2 wyib, P2] to last 3 sts, sl2 wyib, P1.
Row 9: K2, [sl2 wyif, K2] to end of row.
Row 10: P1, [sl2 wyib, P2] rep to last st, P1.
Row 11: Sl2 wyif, [K2, sl2 wyif] to end of row.
Row 12: P3, [sl2 wyib, P2] to last 3 sts, sl2 wyib, P1.
Row 13: Sl2 wyif, [K2, sl2 wyif] to end of row.
Row 14: P1, [sl2 wyib, P2] to last st, P1.
Row 15: K2, [sl2, wyif, K2] to end of row.

Row 16: P3, [sl2 wyib, P2] to last 3 sts, sl2 wyib, P1.
Row 17: Sl2 wyif, [K2, sl2 wyif] to end of row.
Row 18: P1, [sl2 wyib, P2] to last st, P1.
Row 19: K2, [sl2, wyif, K2] to end of row.
Row 20: P3, [sl2 wyib, P2] to last 3 sts, sl2 wyib, P1.
Row 21: Sl2 wyif, [K2, sl2 wyif] to end of row.
Row 22: P1, [sl2 wyib, P2] to last st, P1.
Row 23: K2, [sl2, wyif, K2] to end of row.
Row 24: P3, [sl2 wyib, P2] to last 3 sts, sl2 wyib, P1.
Rep rows 1–24 once more.
Next row: K.
Next row: P.
Next row (RS): K22 and slip these sts onto a holder, P54, K to end of row.
Work the first handle on the last 22 sts as foll:
Starting with a P row, work 31 rows St st, ending with RS facing for next row.
Change to B and starting with a P row, work 26 rows in Rev St st. Slip these sts onto a holder. Cut yarn leaving a long end.
With WS of work facing and **B**, rejoin yarn to centre 54 sts and beg with a P row, work 9 rows in St st. Cast off.
With WS of work facing, rejoin **A** to the 22 sts on the holder and work another handle to match the first handle.
Join both handles using the three-needle cast-off method, with WS tog so that the seam is on the outside of your work.
Rep from * for the other side of the bag.

Finish

Weave any ends in and out of the sts on the WS of the work. Choose a flat padded surface or blocking board and pin work out to measurements. Cover with a damp cloth and gently steam on reverse.
Fold handles in half with WS tog and join seam, allowing top of side to fold back at an angle. Fold knitted black facing strips at top of bag to WS and slip stitch into place.

Lining

Make paper patterns as follows, which have 1cm seam allowances:
Base x 1: 35cm diameter circle.
Sides x 2: 36cm x 50cm. Place markers 15cm from top.

Cut out lining pieces. Join both sides from marker to bottom with 1cm seams. Pin and ease base to fit. Tack and sew with 1cm seam. Fold 1.5cm along top edges of lining to WS. Pin and press. Mark the centre of each side with a pin and do the same for the bag.
With WS tog, insert lining into bag, matching centres. Pin 2cm from the top of the black facing, folding the excess fabric at the corners to the inside to fit under the fold formed by the handles.
Slip stitch all round.
Catch base of lining to knitted base at centre.

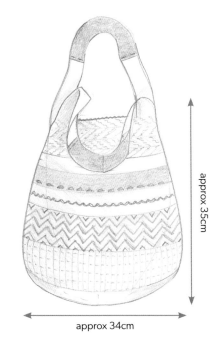

approx 35cm

approx 34cm

lampshade

A Japanese inspired lampshade made from a basic willow frame and a sleeve of fine open knitting stretched over the centre of the frame.

Measurements
One size
Approx. 41cm diameter x 39cm high

Materials
Rowan Kidsilk Haze
70% Mohair, 25% Silk
Approx. 210m per 25g ball
Quantity: 2 balls (photographed in Jelly 597)
5.5mm and 7mm circular needles with 80cm length wire
Stitch marker
Lampshade frame made from natural, flexible willow and masking tape
Large-eyed, blunt-tipped sewing needle
Note: Yarn amounts given are based on average requirements and are approximate.

Tension
Approx. 15 sts and 22 rows to 10cm, meas over St st using 5.5mm needles. Change needle size as necessary to ensure the correct tension.

Abbreviations
See p.70.

Frame

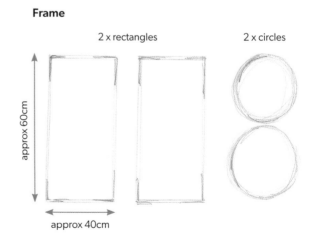

2 x rectangles   2 x circles

approx 60cm

approx 40cm

Make

Using 7mm needles, cast on 193 sts loosely, then place marker to show start of round. Change to 5.5mm circular needle and work in St st – all rounds K – until work meas 39cm from the cast-on, ending at the marker.
Cast off loosely using the 7mm circular needle.

Make the frame

Using natural, flexible willow, create a frame of 2 circles with an inside edge diameter of approx. 40cm and 2 rectangles approx. 40cm wide and 60cm tall, binding the shapes together, as shown in the diagram, and using masking tape at the joining and stress points to stabilise. You may wish to cover the masking tape with linen yarn or string.

Finish

Weave any ends in and out of the sts on the WS of the work. Slide the cast-off edge over the frame and oversew to the bottom ring. Carefully ease out the knitted sleeve and pull the cast-on edge up to the top ring of the frame and oversew to secure.

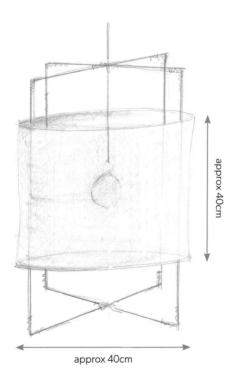

approx 40cm

approx 40cm

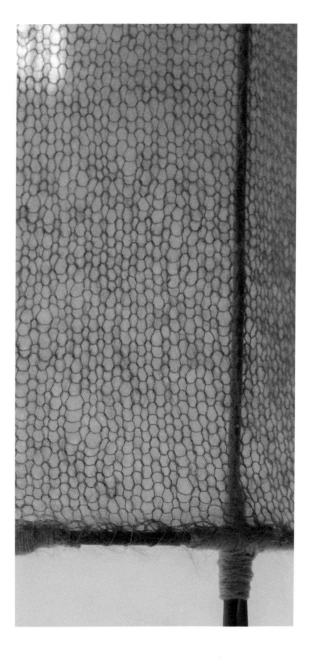

rug

A small rug worked using the yarn held double to create a practical textile. Knitted in a herringbone stitch for a woven look, and finished with short, simple tufts.

Measurements
One size
Approx. 80cm x 50cm

Materials
Rowan Creative Linen
50% Cotton, 50% Linen
Approx. 200m per 100g hank
Quantity: 6 hanks (photographed in Natural 621)
5mm circular needles with 80cm length wire
4.5mm crochet hook (to add tufts)
Large-eyed, blunt-tipped sewing needle
Note: Yarn amounts given are based on average requirements and are approximate.

Tension
20 sts and 26 rows to 10cm, meas over pattern using 5mm needles with yarn held double. Change needle size as necessary to ensure the correct tension.

Note
Yarn used double throughout.
This pattern uses circular needles to work in rows. (See p.70)

Abbreviations
See p.70.

Special abbreviations
Sl slip stitch purlwise
Wyif with yarn in front
Wyib with yarn in back

Make

Using 5mm needles and yarn used double, cast on 158 sts and work in herringbone pattern as foll:

Row 1 (RS): K2, [sl2 wyif, K2] to end of row.
Row 2: P1, [sl2 wyib, P2] rep to last st, P1.
Row 3: Sl2 wyif, [K2, sl2 wyif] to end of row.
Row 4: P3, [sl2 wyib, P2] to last 3 sts, sl2 wyib, P1.
Row 5: K2, [sl2 wyif, K2] to end of row.
Row 6: P1, [sl2 wyib, P2] rep to last st, P1.
Row 7: Sl2 wyif, [K2, sl2 wyif] to end of row.
Row 8: P3, [sl2 wyib, P2] to last 3 sts, sl2 wyib, P1.
Row 9: K2, [sl2 wyif, K2] to end of row.
Row 10: P1, [sl2 wyib, P2] rep to last st, P1.
Row 11: Sl2 wyif, [K2, sl2 wyif] to end of row.
Row 12: P3, [sl2 wyib, P2] to last 3 sts, sl2 wyib, P1.
Row 13: Sl2 wyif, [K2, sl2 wyif] to end of row.
Row 14: P1, [sl2 wyib, P2] to last st, P1.
Row 15: K2, [sl2, wyif, K2] to end of row.
Row 16: P3, [sl2 wyib, P2] to last 3 sts, sl2 wyib, P1.
Row 17: Sl2 wyif, [K2, sl2 wyif] to end of row.
Row 18: P1, [sl2 wyib, P2] to last st, P1.
Row 19: K2, [sl2, wyif, K2] to end of row.
Row 20: P3, [sl2 wyib, P2] to last 3 sts, sl2 wyib, P1.
Row 21: Sl2 wyif, [K2, sl2 wyif] to end of row.
Row 22: P1, [sl2 wyib, P2] to last st, P1.
Row 23: K2, [sl2, wyif, K2] to end of row.
Row 24: P3, [sl2 wyib, P2] to last 3 sts, sl2 wyib, P1.
Rep these 24 rows 7 times more.
Cast off in pattern.

Finish

Weave any ends in and out of the sts on the WS of the work. With remaining yarn, cut lengths of approx. 18cm and leave to one side.

Push the crochet hook up through a stitch along the edge of the rug. Take 2 of the lengths of yarn and fold them in half. Using the crochet hook pull the yarn down half-way through the stitch, then take the loop and pull the ends through to secure. Repeat at approx. 5cm intervals around the edge of the rug and at each corner. Trim to approx. 4cm, or as desired.

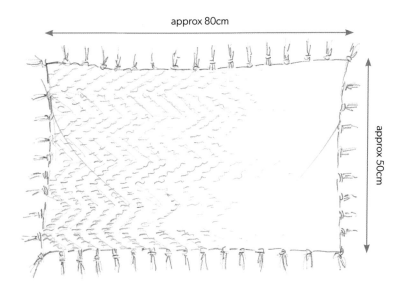

approx 80cm

approx 50cm

bobble pot

A pot cover or plant holder knitted in the round using the yarn held double, with contemporary texture created by tactile bobbles.

Measurements
One size
Approx. 15.5cm diameter x 16cm high

Materials
Rowan Creative Linen
50% Cotton, 50% Linen
Approx. 200m per 100g hank
Quantity: 1 hank (photographed in Natural 621)
5mm circular needles with 60cm length wire
Stitch marker
Large-eyed, blunt-tipped sewing needle
Note: Yarn amounts given are based on average requirements and are approximate.

Tension
16 sts and 22 rows to 10cm, meas over St st using 5mm needles with yarn held double. Change needle size as necessary to ensure the correct tension.
Note
Yarn used double throughout.
The magic loop technique is used for the base. (See p.70)

Abbreviations
See p.70.

Special abbreviations
kfb knit into front and back of next st.
MB (Make Bobble) [K1, P1] twice into next st, turn and P4, turn and K4, then with left needle, lift 2nd, 3rd and 4th sts over the first stitch on the right needle.

Make

With yarn held double throughout, cast on 8 sts, place marker to show the start of the round and, making sure that the cast-on row is not twisted, work in rounds as foll:

Round 1: K.
Round 2: kfb into each st. 16 sts.
Round 3: K.
Round 4: [K1, kfb] to end of round. 24 sts.
Round 5: K.
Round 6: [K2, kfb] to end of round. 32 sts.
Round 7: K.
Round 8: [K3, kfb] to end of round. 40 sts.
Round 9: K.
Round 10: [K4, kfb] to end of round. 48 sts.
Round 11: K.
Round 12: [K5, kfb] to end of round. 56 sts.
Round 13: K.
Round 14: [K6, kfb] to end of round. 64 sts.
Work 7 rounds straight.
Next round: [MB, K3] to end of round.
Work 6 rounds straight.
Rep last 7 rounds three times more.
Next round: P.
Cast off in K.

Finish

Weave any ends in and out of the sts on the WS of the work.

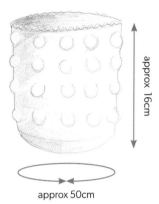

approx 16cm

approx 50cm

pot

A plain stocking stitch version of the plant pot.

Measurements
One size
Approx. 10.5cm diameter x 12.5cm high

Materials
Rowan Creative Linen
50% Cotton, 50% Linen
Approx. 200m per 100g hank
Quantity: 1 hank (photographed in Natural 621)
5mm circular needle with 60cm length wire
Stitch marker
Large-eyed, blunt-tipped sewing needle
Note: Yarn amounts given are based on average requirements and are approximate.

Tension
16 sts and 22 rows to 10cm, meas over St st using 5mm needles with yarn held double. Change needle size as necessary to ensure the correct tension.

Note
Yarn used double throughout.
The magic loop technique is used for the base. (See p.70)

Abbreviations
See p.70.

Special abbreviations
kfb knit into front and back of next st.
M1 make 1 st by picking up and knitting into back of loop between st just worked and next st.

Make

Using 5mm needles and yarn used double, cast on 8 sts, place marker to show the start of the round and, making sure that the cast-on row is not twisted, work in rounds as foll:

Round 1: K.
Round 2: kfb into each st. 16 sts.
Round 3: K.
Round 4: [K1, kfb] to end of round. 24 sts.
Round 5: K.
Round 6: [K2, kfb] to end of round. 32 sts.
Round 7: K.
Round 8: [K3, kfb] to end of round. 40 sts.
Round 9: K.
Round 10: [K4, kfb] to end of round. 48 sts.
Work 6 rounds straight.
Next round (inc): [K12, M1] to end of round. 52 sts
Work 27 rounds straight.
Next round: P.
Cast off in K.

Finish

Weave any ends in and out of the sts on the WS of the work.

approx 12.5cm

approx 33cm

cell stitch cushions

Use the same open work stitch in a different weight or fibre to create very simple squares for textural cushions.

Big Wool Cushion
Materials
Rowan Big Wool
100% Wool
Approx. 80m per 100g ball
Quantity: 3 balls (photographed in Cactus 083)
7mm needles
50cm x 50cm cushion pad
Linen fabric for backing approx. 60cm x 75cm
Large-eyed, blunt-tipped sewing needle
Note: Yarn amounts given are based on average requirements and are approximate.

Creative Linen Cushion
Materials
Rowan Creative Linen
50% Cotton, 50% Linen
Approx. 200m per 100g hank
Quantity: 2 hanks (photographed in Straw 622)
3.75mm needles
40cm x 40cm cushion pad
Linen fabric for backing approx. 50cm x 70cm
Large-eyed, blunt-tipped sewing needle
Note: Yarn amounts given are based on average requirements and are approximate.

Tension
Big Wool
13 sts and 16 rows to 10cm, meas over pattern using 7mm needles. Change needle size as necessary to ensure the correct tension.
Creative Linen
21 sts and 28 rows to 10cm, meas over pattern using 3.75mm needles. Change needle size as necessary to ensure the correct tension.

Abbreviations
See p.70.

Special abbreviations
Skpo slip 1 st knitwise, K1, pass slipped stitch over.
Sk2po slip 1 st knitwise, K2tog, pass slipped stitch over.

Make

Cell stitch pattern multiple of 4 + 3 sts.
Row 1 (RS): K2, [yf, Sk2po, yf, K1], rep to last st, K1.
Row 2: P.
Row 3: K1, K2tog, yf, K1, [yf, Sk2po, yf, K1], rep to last 3 sts, yf, Skpo, K1.
Row 4: P.
Rep these 4 rows.

Big Wool Cushion
Using 7mm needles, cast on 59 sts and work the cell stitch pattern until work meas 50cm from the cast-on edge.
Cast off.

Creative Linen Cushion
Using 3.75mm needles, cast on 83 sts and work the cell stitch pattern until work meas 40cm from the cast-on edge.
Cast off.

Finish
Weave any ends in and out of the sts on the WS of the work. Choose a flat padded surface or blocking board and pin work out to measurements. Cover with a damp cloth and gently steam. Leave to dry flat.
Make fabric back. See p.64.

Creative Linen Cushion

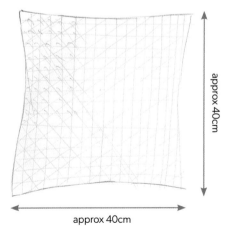

approx 40cm

approx 40cm

Big Wool Cushion

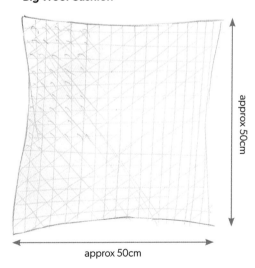

approx 50cm

approx 50cm

tassel cushion

A simple cushion knitted in stocking stitch and reverse stocking stitch in stripes and bands of colour and texture, embellished with basic embroidery and with tassels in each corner.

Measurements
One size
Approx. 50cm x 30cm

Materials
Rowan Creative Linen
50% Cotton, 50% Linen
Approx. 200m per 100g hank
Quantity:
A 2 hanks (photographed in Straw 622)
B 1 hank (photographed in True Black 653)
Rowan Felted Tweed Aran
50% Wool, 25% Viscose, 25% Alpaca
Approx. 87m per 50g ball
Quantity:
C 1 ball (photographed in Treacle 783)
D 1 ball (photographed in Cinnamon 780)
4mm needles
30cm x 50cm cushion pad
Linen fabric for backing approx. 50cm x 70cm
Large-eyed, blunt-tipped sewing needle
Note: Yarn amounts given are based on average requirements and are approximate.

Tension
20 sts and 29 rows to 10cm, meas over St st using 4mm needles and Creative Linen. Change needle size as necessary to ensure the correct tension.

Notes

Joining in new colours
On row before you need the new colour, work to the last stitch. Taking the end of the new colour, use together with the yarn in work to work the last stitch, creating a 'double stitch'. On the first stitch of the next row, work the double stitch as one stitch with just the end of the new colour. This will securely 'anchor' your new yarn and not create unsightly knots nor create bumps.

Weaving in ends should be done along the fabric, never along the side edge.

Abbreviations
See p.70.

Make

Using 4mm needles and yarn **A**, cast on 56 sts and beg with a K row, cont in St st until work meas 8cm from the cast-on, ending with WS facing for next row.

Change to **B** and P to end of row.

Change to **A** and beg with a K row, cont in St st until work meas 12.5cm from the cast-on, ending with RS facing for next row.

Change to **C** and P to end of row, then K the next row.

Change to **A** and P to end of row.

Still using **A** and starting with a P row, cont in St st until work meas 18.5cm from the cast-on edge, ending with RS facing for next row.

Change to **B** and K to end of row.

Change to **A** and beg with a P row, cont in St st until work meas 26cm from the cast-on, ending with RS facing for next row.

Change to **D** and cont in St st until work meas 35cm from the cast-on edge, ending with RS facing for next row.

Change to **A** and cont in St st until work meas 48cm from the cast-on, ending with RS facing for next row.

Cast off.

Finish

Weave any ends in and out of the sts on the WS of the work. Choose a flat padded surface or blocking board and pin work out to measurements. Cover with a damp cloth and gently steam. Leave to dry flat.

Make fabric back. See p.64.

Using **B** and a large-eyed, blunt-tipped needle, embellish the RS of the cushion with strong uneven lines either side of the broad tweed band as an additional detail. See photo.

Using the leftover yarn, cut 8 lengths approx. 30cm long each and leave to one side. Take a paperback book and wrap the leftover yarn approximately 30 times around the length of the book. Cut the end of the yarn and gently slide the looped bundle off the book, holding it in the middle. Take a 30cm length of yarn and fold it in half. Lay the looped bundle on the folded yarn length and tie it up by threading the ends through the loop. Pull up tightly and knot securely. This will be the thread with which to fasten on to the cushion. Take another 30cm length and tie around the looped bundle approx. 2.5cm down from the hanging thread. Wind the ends around to secure the bundle, tuck in the ends, knot and trim off. Cut through the loops at the end of the bundle, trim and gently shake out to create a tassel. Make 3 more in the same way, and fasten each to a corner of the cushion using the long thread.

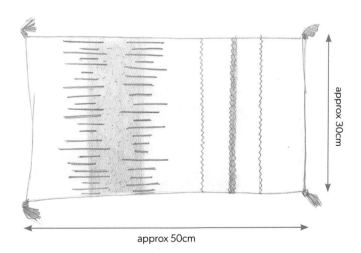

approx 30cm

approx 50cm

stripe cushion

A simple cushion worked in textures of linen and tweed, knitted in stripes and blocks of colour in stocking stitch and reverse stocking stitch, allowing the colour change rows to provide further detail.

Measurements
One size
Approx. 45cm x 45cm

Materials
Rowan Creative Linen
50% Cotton, 50% Linen
Approx. 200m per 100g hank
Quantity:
A 2 balls (photographed in Natural 621)
Rowan Felted Tweed Aran
50% Wool, 25% Viscose, 25% Alpaca
Approx. 87m per 50g ball
Quantity:
B 1 ball (photographed in Treacle 783)
4mm needles
45cm x 45cm cushion pad
Linen fabric for backing approx. 50cm x 75cm
Large-eyed, blunt-tipped sewing needle
Note: Yarn amounts given are based on average requirements and are approximate.

Tension
20 sts and 29 rows to 10cm, meas over St st using 4mm needles and Creative Linen. Change needle size as necessary to ensure the correct tension.

Notes

Joining in new colours
On row before you need the new colour, work to the last stitch. Taking the end of the new colour, use together with the yarn in work to work the last stitch, creating a 'double stitch'. On the first stitch of the next row, work the double stitch as one stitch with just the end of the new colour. This will securely 'anchor' your new yarn and not create unsightly knots nor create bumps.

Weaving in ends, should be done along the fabric, never along the side edge.

Abbreviations
See p.70.

Make

Using 4mm needles and **A**, cast on 88 sts.

Beg with a K row, work 7cm in St st, ending with WS facing for next row.

Change to **B** and K to end of row.

Change to **A** and beg with a K row, cont in St st until work meas 16cm from the cast-on, ending with RS facing for next row.

Change to **B** and beg with a P row, cont in Rev St st until work meas 19.5cm from the cast-on, ending with RS facing for next row.

Change to **A** and P to end of row. Then beg with a P row, cont in St st until work meas 22cm from the cast-on, ending with RS facing for next row.

Change to **B** and work in St st until work meas 24.5cm from the cast-on, ending with RS facing for next row.

Change to **A** and work 2 rows St st.

Change to **B** and work in St st until work meas 34cm from the cast-on, ending with RS facing for next row.

Change to **A** and work in St st until work meas 38cm from the cast-on, ending with RS facing for next row.

Change to **B** and P to end of row.

Change to **A** and beg with a P row, cont in St st until work meas 44cm from the cast-on edge, ending with RS facing for next row.

Cast off.

Finish

Weave any ends in and out of the sts on the WS of the work. Choose a flat padded surface or blocking board and pin work out to measurements. Cover with a damp cloth and gently steam. Leave to dry flat.

Make fabric back. See p.64.

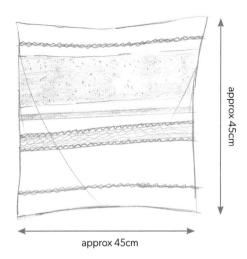

approx 45cm

approx 45cm

trellis stitch cushion

A simple cushion knitted in an exaggerated trellis stitch and made with a linen fabric back.

Measurements
One size
Approx. 40cm x 40cm

Materials
Rowan Creative Linen
50% Cotton, 50% Linen
Approx. 200m per 100g hank
Quantity: 2 hanks (photographed in Natural 621)
4mm needles
Stitch marker
40cm x 40cm cushion pad
Linen fabric for backing approx. 50cm x 70cm
Large-eyed, blunt-tipped sewing needle
Note: Yarn amounts given are based on average requirements and are approximate.

Tension
19 sts and 26 rows to 10cm, meas over pattern using 4mm needles. Change needle size as necessary to ensure the correct tension.

Notes
Inc in first st - knit into front and back of first st.
Picking up stitches with WS facing – with the WS of work facing, insert the RH needle through the edge of the fabric from **back to front,** wind yarn around the needle and draw the loop through, forming a stitch on the RH needle.
Cont in this way until the required number of stitches is on the RH needle.

Abbreviations
See p.70.

Make
Large trellis pattern multiple of 24 sts for this cushion.
Using 4mm needles, cast on 48 sts loosely and place a marker after 24 sts. This marks the base triangles and can be removed when the base triangles are completed.

Base triangles
*P2 (WS), turn and K2, turn and P3, turn and K3, turn and P4, turn and K4, cont in this way working 1 more st on every WS row until the row 'turn and P24' has been worked. (This completes the first triangle over 24 sts.) Rep from * to end.

First row of rectangles (with edge triangles)
K2, turn and P2, turn, inc in first st, K2tog tbl, turn and P3, turn, inc in first st, K1, K2tog tbl, turn and P4, turn, inc in first st, K2, K2tog tbl, turn and P5, turn, inc in first st, K3, K2tog tbl, turn and P6, cont in this way working one more st on every RS row until the row 'inc in first st, K21, K2tog tbl' has been worked. (1 edge triangle complete), then cont as foll:
With the RS facing, pick up and K 24 sts evenly along edge of next base triangle [turn and P24, turn and K23, K2tog tbl] 24 times (1 rectangle complete).
With the RS facing, pick up and K24 sts along edge of last triangle, turn and P2tog, P22 turn and K23, turn and P2tog, P21, turn. Cont in this way until 'turn and K2' has been worked, turn and P2tog (1 st remains on RH needle and edge triangle is complete).

Second row of rectangles
Continuing from the st on RH needle, with the WS facing, pick up and P23 sts evenly along edge of triangle just worked (24 sts on RH needle), [turn and K24, turn and P23, P2tog] 24 times, then cont as foll:
With the WS facing, pick up and P24 sts evenly along side edge of next rectangle, [turn and K24, turn and P23, P2tog] 24 times.

Third row of rectangles
As first row but picking up sts along side edge of rectangles instead of triangles.

Final row of triangles
*Cont on from st on RH needle, with the WS facing, pick up and P23 sts evenly along edge of triangle just worked, turn and K24, turn and P2tog, P21, P2tog, turn and K23, turn and P2tog, P20, P2tog, turn and K22, turn.
Cont in this way, working one st less on every WS row until the row 'turn and K3' has been worked, turn and [P2tog] twice, turn and K2, turn and P1, P2tog, P1, turn and K3, turn and P3tog; rep from * but pick up sts along side edge of rectangle instead of triangle. Fasten off rem st.

Finish
Weave any ends in and out of the sts on the WS of the work. Choose a flat padded surface or blocking board and pin work out to measurements. Cover with a damp cloth and gently steam. Leave to dry flat.
Make fabric back. See p.64.

approx 40cm

approx 40cm

fabric envelope back for all cushions

Cut 2 rectangles
Width = ½ a + 12cm
Length = b + 2cm
1cm seam allowances are included.

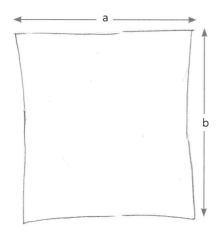

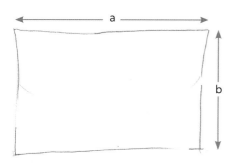

Make a narrow double hem along one long edge of
each rectangle for the square cushions and along
one short edge of each rectangle for the rectangular
tassel cushion.

Block and steam knitting, then lay flat with RS facing
you. Place one back piece RS down to the right of your
knitting, matching edges. Place the second piece to
the left so that the hemmed edges overlap.

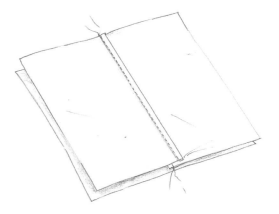

Pin and tack around all edges. Sew taking a 1cm
seam allowance.

Turn and insert cushion pad.

wall hanging

A large piece of knitting worked in rows of texture stitch patterns using the yarn held double and large needles so that the stitches are exaggerated. Do not cast off, but thread the stitches on a rod to hang on a wall inside, and add fringe to detail.

Measurements
One size
Approx. 45cm x 65cm

Materials
Rowan Creative Linen
50% Cotton, 50% Linen
Approx. 200m per 100g hank
Quantity: 2 hanks (photographed in Natural 621)
10mm needles
Large cable needle
10mm crochet hook (to add fringing)
Stick, bamboo or metal rod for hanging
Large-eyed, blunt-tipped sewing needle
Note: Yarn amounts given are based on average requirements and are approximate.

Tension
11 sts and 12 rows to 10cm, meas over St st using 10mm needles with two ends of the yarn held together. Change needle size as necessary to ensure the correct tension.

Note
Yarn used double throughout.

Abbreviations
See p.70.

Special abbreviations
C3B (Cable 3 Back) slip next st onto cable needle and hold at back of work, knit next 2 sts from left-hand needle, then knit st from cable needle.
C3F (Cable 3 Front) slip next 2 sts onto cable needle and hold at front of work, knit next st from left-hand needle, then knit sts from cable needle.
C4B (Cable 4 Back) slip next 2 sts onto cable needle and hold at back of work, knit next 2 sts from left-hand needle, then knit sts from cable needle.

Make

Using 10mm needles and yarn used double, cast on 76 sts and work in garter drop stitch as foll:

Rows 1-4: K.

Row 5: *K1 winding yarn twice around needle; rep from * to end of row.

Row 6: K to end, dropping the extra loops.

Rows 7-9: K.

Row 10: P.

Cont in fancy openwork as foll:

Row 1 (RS): K2, *yf, K4; rep from * to last 2 sts, yf, K2.

Row 2: P2tog, *[K1, P1] into the yf of the previous row, [P2tog] twice; rep from * to last 3 sts, [K1, P1] into the yf, P2tog.

Row 3: K4, *yf, K4; rep from * to end.

Row 4: P2, P2tog, *[K1, P1] into the yf of the previous row, [P2tog] twice; rep from * to last 5 sts, [K1, P1] into the yf, P2tog, P2.

Cont in crossed diamond cable as foll:

Row 1 (RS): K2tog, K3, C3B, C3F, *K6, C3B, C3F; rep from * to last 5 sts, K3, K2tog. 74 sts.

Row 2: P.

Row 3: K3, C3B, K2, C3F, *K4, C3B, K2, C3F; rep from * to last 3 sts, K3.

Row 4: P.

Row 5: *K2, C3B, K4, C3F; rep from * to last 2 sts, K2.

Row 6: P.

Row 7: K1, *C3B, K6, C3F; rep from * to last st, K1.

Row 8: P.

Row 9: K11, *C4B, K8; rep from * to last 3 sts, K3.

Row 10: P.

Row 11: K1, *C3F, K6, C3B; rep from * to last st, K1.

Row 12: P

Row 13: *K2, C3F, K4, C3B; rep from * to last 2 sts, K2.

Row 14: P.

Row 15: K3, C3F, K2, C3B, *K4, C3F, K2, C3B; rep from * to last 3 sts, K3.

Row 16: P.

Row 17: K4, C3F, C3B, *K6, C3F, C3B; rep from * to last 4 sts, K4.

Row 18: P.

Row 19: K5, C4B, *K8, C4B; rep from * to last 5 sts, K5.

Row 20: P.

Cont in garter drop stitch as foll:

Next row: [K1 winding yarn twice around needle] 28 times, [K1 winding yarn once around needle] 13 times, [K1 winding yarn twice around needle] 15 times, [K1 winding yarn once around needle] 13 times and [K1 winding yarn twice around needle] 5 times.

Next row: K to end of row dropping the extra loops.

Cont in bramble stitch as foll:

Row 1 (RS): P.

Row 2: K1, *[K1, P1, K1] into next st, P3tog; rep from * to last st, K1.

Row 3: P.

Row 4: K1, *P3tog, [K1, P1, K1] into next st; rep from * to last st, K1.

Work 5 rows K.

Finish

Cut yarn leaving a long end.

Slip the stitches onto a rod for hanging.

Weave in any ends.

Using yarn held double, cut lengths of approx. 43cm and leave to one side.

With RS facing and starting at the left-hand bottom edge, insert the crochet hook up through the centre of the first stitch along the edge of the piece. Take two of the lengths of yarn and fold them in half. Using the crochet hook, draw the centre of the folded yarn down half-way through the stitch. Remove the hook and pass the yarn ends through the loop created. Pull the yarn ends gently to tighten the loop. Repeat on every other stitch along the bottom edge of the piece. Trim to approx. 15cm, or as desired.

approx 45cm

approx 65cm

This oversized swatch is a place to channel your thought process, or simply to try out a few new stitch techniques. Focus on the creative journey and take a pause in the spaces between stitches. Making by hand is an extension of you; honour your craft by displaying your handiwork proudly on the wall.

ABBREVIATIONS

[ ]	work instructions within square brackets as many times as directed.
( )	work instructions within round brackets for your chosen size.
Alt	alternate.
Beg	begin(ning).
cm	centimetre(s).
Col	colour.
Cont	continue.
Dec	decrease.
Foll(s)	follow(s)(ing).
g	gram(s).
Inc	increase.
K	knit.
kfb	knit into front and back of next st.
K2tog	knit 2 sts together.
m	metre(s).
MB	make bobble - [K1, P1] twice into next st, turn and P4, turn and K4, then with left needle lift 2nd, 3rd and 4th sts over the first stitch on the right needle.
Meas	measure(s).
M1	make 1 st by picking up and knitting into back of loop between st just worked and next st.
P	purl.
Patt	pattern.
P2tog	purl 2 sts together.
Psso	pass slipped stitch over.
Rem	remain(ing).
Rep	repeat.
Rev St st	reverse stocking stitch.
RH	right hand.
RS	right side.
Sl	slip stitch.
Skpo	slip 1 st knitwise, k1, pass slipped stitch over – a one stitch decrease.
St(s)	stitch(es).
St st	stocking stitch.
Tbl	through back of loop.
Tog	together.
WS	wrong side.
Wyib	with yarn in back.
Wyif	with yarn in front.
yd(s)	yard(s).
Yf	yarn forward.
Yo	yarn over.

TENSION

The ball band around the yarn should give you all the tension information you require: how many stitches and rows the yarn will knit per centimetre or inch, usually worked over stocking stitch using a specified needle. You can use this tension information to choose a matching substitute yarn, if you wish to use a yarn you already have in your stash. Each pattern will also state a tension, which has been used for the specific design to achieve the desired knitted fabric. The tension determines the measurements of a garment, so always check your tension before you begin a project to ensure you obtain the same number of rows and stitches as the pattern states. Using the same yarn and needles and stitch that the tension has been measured over in the pattern, knit a small swatch at least 13cm square.

TECHNIQUES

WORKING IN ROWS WITH CIRCULAR NEEDLES

Used for projects like the stitch throw, patchwork blanket and bag. For ease and comfort, circular needles are used to work in rows (flat knitting).

1. Cast on the required number of stitches. Slide the stitches onto the wire of the needle.

2. Hold the needle end with the stitches on it in your left hand and the empty end in your right. Work across all the stitches.

3. To work the next row, swap the needle ends around so that the working yarn is attached to the needle in your left hand. Continue as the pattern requires.

MAGIC LOOP

Used for projects like the bag and pot.

1. Cast on the required number of stitches on one circular needle. Slide the stitches to the wire of the needle. Slide the points of the needles so that each point holds half of the cast-on stitches. Be sure that the working yarn is on the back needle.

2. Join ends to begin working in the round. The back stitches are on the wire and the front stitches on the left needle point, with the right needle point ready to knit the front stitches. The working yarn is at the back and wrapped, ready to knit.

3. Knit across the front stitches, slide the back stitches to the needle point, and turn the work. The first half of the stitches have been knitted. The second half of the stitches are pushed to the point and the work is turned.

4. Slide the stitches just knitted to the wire and begin to knit the second half of the stitches (now on the front needle).

SIZING

For the homeware projects in this book, the patterns are written for one size, as stated at the beginning of each pattern. For the two wearable garments, however, there are a choice of nine sizes. Measurements are provided at the beginning of the pattern for each size. In addition to this, there is a schematic drawing which shows the dimensions of the design's pieces before they are sewn together, with the different sizes shown (in parenthesis). The schematic will help you to assess the fit and ease of the design in order to make a choice about which size to knit to ensure a good fit. It is important to note the finished measurements of the pattern, and to measure yourself, or choose a favourite sweater or t-shirt that you feel comfortable in and that fits you well, lay it out flat and measure.

HOW TO MEASURE

Chest – measure under your arms around the fullest part of your chest.

Length – measure from the centre of the back of your neck to your natural waistline, or from the top of the shoulder to the hem of your favourite sweater.

Waist – measure around your natural waistline below your ribcage, leaving the tape measure a little loose.

Hips – measure around the fullest part of your body, above the top of your legs.

Sleeve length – with arm slightly bent, measure from your armpit to your wrist.

Select an appropriate size to make and knit a tension swatch to ensure you are achieving the same tension as stated in the pattern.
Achieving the right fit for you is one of the benefits of making something by hand, creating a garment that is bespoke and made by you, for you.

FINISHING

Having invested in yarn and many hours of knitting, your hand-crafted project deserves to be finished beautifully. These are some of my favourite techniques for creating a neat, professional finish, and used for the projects in this book.

Three-needle cast-off

1. Hold the two needles with the live stitches parallel to each other in your left hand, with the wrong sides of the knitting facing each other.
2. Knit the first stitch from each needle together with a third needle.
3. Knit the next stitch from each needle together.
4. Pass the first stitch knit over the second stitch.
5. Repeat steps 2 and 3 until all stitches have been cast off.

Invisible seam

1. With the right side of both pieces facing you, secure the yarn to the edge of one piece.
2. Take the needle across to the opposite edge, pick up the equivalent stitch on this piece, pull the yarn through; take the needle back to the first edge, returning the needle through the hole of the previous stitch, then pick up the next stitch and pull the yarn through.
3. Continue in this way, picking up and pulling together stitch to stitch (row for row) along the length of the seam.

Backstitch

1. Place the pieces with the right sides together. Work along the wrong side of the fabric one stitch from the edge. Secure the yarn and work from right to left.
2. With the needle at the back of the work, move along to the left of the length of one knitted stitch, bring the needle back through fabric to front and pull the yarn through.
3. Take the needle from left to right across the front of work to the end of last stitch, insert the needle through the fabric to the back of the work and pull the yarn through.
4. Continue in this way to the end.

CARING FOR YOUR HANDKNITS

When you have devoted so much time in crafting a handknit, it is important to care for it to ensure a long life. Homeware and outerwear garments may not need laundering on a regular basis.

Wash

Always check the ball band of the yarn you have used for specific washing instructions. Not all yarns are machine washable. Hand washing is usually the safest and gentlest way to wash your handknits. Use lukewarm water (never hot, as this can cause natural fibres to 'felt') and choose a specially formulated detergent for wool and delicates. You may wish to use your tension swatch to test how your project will react to washing.

Dry

Gently squeeze out any excess water, leave to dry flat on top of an absorbent towel, and away from direct heat, easing the garment back to its original shape.

Store

Handknits should be stored folded rather than hanging and in an airtight container if possible, as natural fibres and body oil can attract destructive moths.

Repair

Over the lifetime of your handknit, small areas of wear and tear will inevitably occur. These can be mended invisibly in the same yarn and colour by darning, or you can choose to use a visible darning method in a contrasting colour to accentuate the repair and make a feature of it.

erika knight

Having honed her craft through a career spanning fashion, education and knitwear, Erika Knight has always had a passion for the handmade, celebrating that creative urge that stirs us to knit, stitch and make. Returning to the tactile mark making that characterised her earliest endeavours as a Fine Art student, Erika's designs are first and foremost about texture and fibre, keeping it simple and finding enjoyment in the process of creating. The projects in this book are both practical in their outcome and purposeful in the mindful activity of their creation.

knit,
stitch
and make.

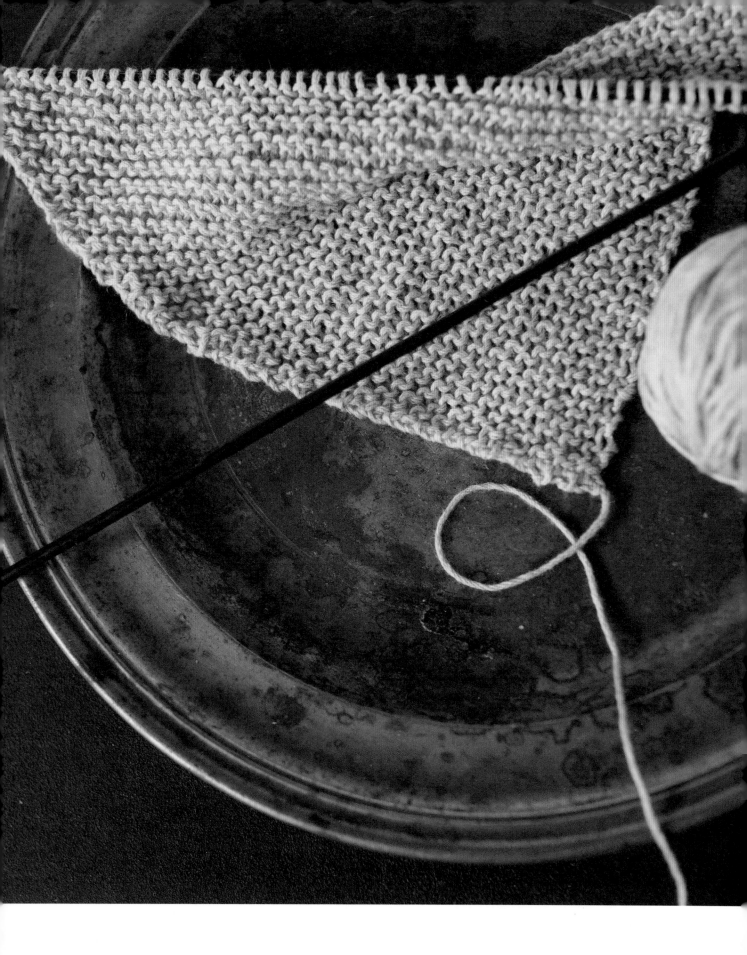

acknowledgements

YARN
The yarns used for all the projects in this book are
Rowan Yarns.
For a full list of stockists and to find a local store or
online retailer, please visit
www.knitrowan.com

BUTTONS
For a beautiful selection of buttons,
please visit
www.textilegarden.com

LOCATION AND PROPS
Thank you to Adele and Hélène of Freight HHG for sharing
their wonderful space in Lewes, East Sussex, along with their
carefully considered homewares.
To find out more, please visit
www.freightstore.co.uk

Thank you to the extraordinary team of women who have collaborated

in challenging circumstances to create this book,

mostly from their own homes, and to Darren at

Quail Publishing for his encouragement and belief in this project.

This book is dedicated to all knitters. BUY LESS AND KNIT MORE.

Q
quail publishing